My Life as a Baby

THIS IS MY STORY!

My Name _____

My Birthdate _____

 Peter Pauper Press, Inc. • White Plains, New York

By Virginia Reynolds
Illustrated by Amy Dietrich
Designed by Heather Zschock

Illustrations copyright © 2001 Amy Dietrich
Text copyright © 2001
Peter Pauper Press, Inc.
202 Mamaroneck Avenue
White Plains, NY 10601

ISBN 978-0-88088-667-3
Printed on acid-free paper
Printed in China
35   34   33   32   31   30   29
Visit us at www.peterpauper.com

Contents

All About My Family

I am _____ 's and

_____ 's pride and joy.

_____

I'm the apple of everybody's eye (of course!), but especially

_____

(Maternal Grandmother)

_____

(Maternal Grandfather)

_____

(Paternal Grandmother)

_____

(Paternal Grandfather)

_____

_____

Photo of Me! (Wasn't I the cutest?)

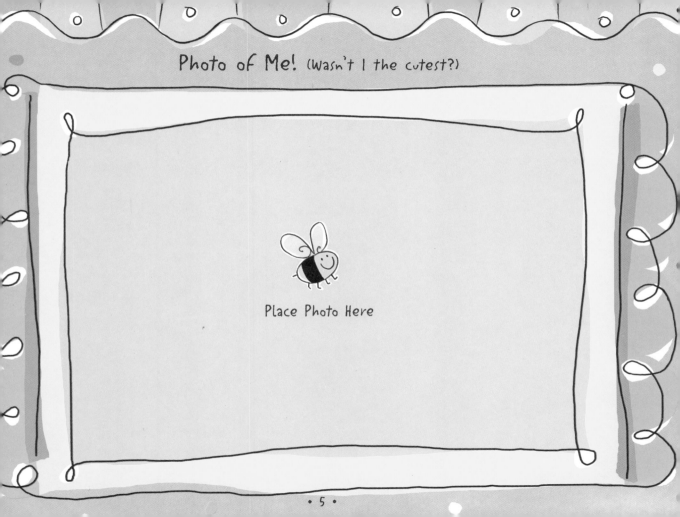

Place Photo Here

My Vital Statistics

Important stuff to record for posterity (whatever that is)

I was born at
_____
(Time)

in
_____
(Hospital/Place)

on
_____
(Date)

I weighed _____ and I was _____ long

☐ I had hair. It was _____
(Color)

☐ I was bald as an egg

My eyes were an enchanting shade of _____

I was especially cute because _____

_____

☐ They said I looked perfect   ☐ They hoped I would grow into my looks

Place Newborn Photo Here

I was born

☐ Head First   ☐ Feet First   ☐ Just like Julius Caesar

People who were there when I made my debut include

Doctor

Nurse

Nurse

Moral support for Mom and Dad

The First thing my mother said when she saw me was
_____

_____

_____

The First thing my father said when he saw me was
_____

_____

_____

They all say I look like
_____

_____

_____

The doctor said that I was
_____

_____

_____

The Early Days

Some of the very special people who visited me were

First Family Photo (I'm the adorable one!)

Place Photo Here

Mom and I went home from the hospital on
_____

_____

We live at
_____
(Address)
_____

_____

_____

The people and pets waiting to welcome us were
_____

_____

_____

_____

_____

_____

Photo of the Star (I can't believe they dressed me up in THAT!)

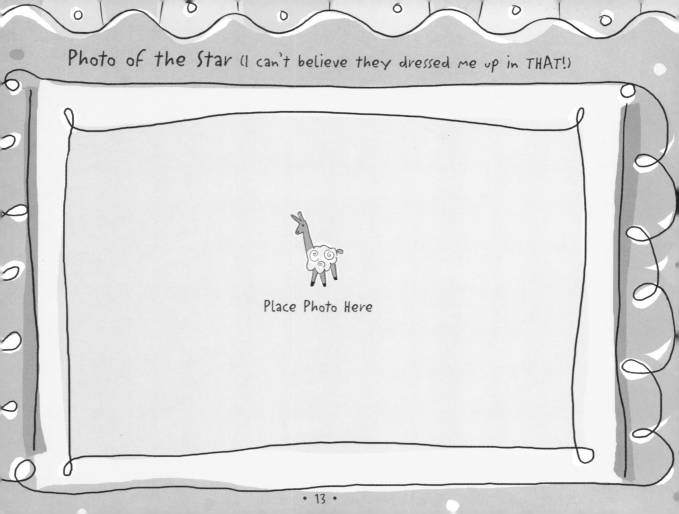

Place Photo Here

The World Around Me When I Was Born

The leader of my country was _____

The big news story of the day (besides my birth) was _____

_____

_____

Movie that won the most awards was _____

Popular songs were _____

_____

Hottest toy in the stores was _____

Price of one package of disposable diapers was $ _____

_____

My World

Place Photo of
Nursery Room/House Here

All About Me

My favorite blanket/comfort object was

I loved to play with

I looked so cute when I wore

I liked to go in the baby carriage to

People other than my parents who took care of me were
_____

_____

_____

My first friends and playmates were
_____

_____

_____

_____

_____

_____

_____

_____

Glad Baby

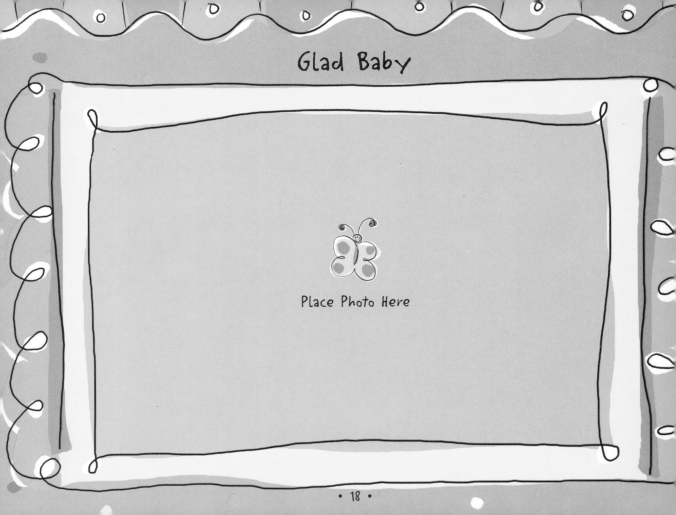

Place Photo Here

Mad Baby

Place Photo Here

Special Event Commemorating My Birth

Christening, Naming, Bris, or Other Special Event was _____

_____

_____

It happened on _____
(Date)

People who shared my special event were _____

_____

_____

_____

_____

_____

That's Me!

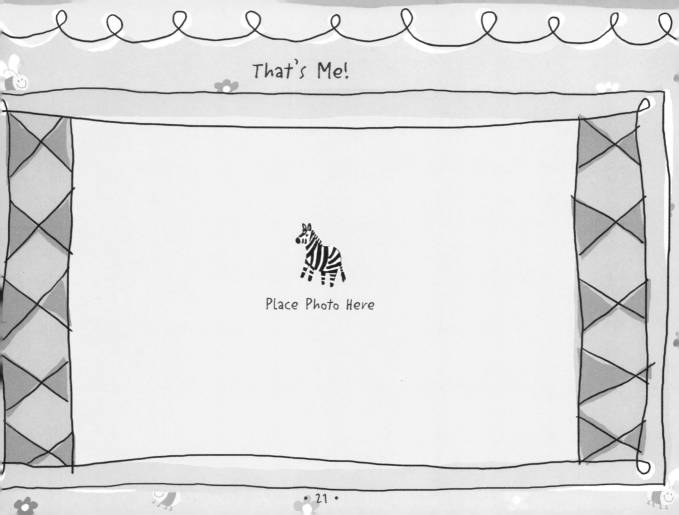

Place Photo Here

Amazing Things About Me

I loved it when Mom
_____

_____

I loved it when Dad
_____

_____

I always smiled at
_____

_____

I always giggled when
_____

_____

I sometimes cried when
_____

_____

The first solid food I ate was

_____

Date

☐ I loved it   ☐ hated it   ☐ spit it out

_____

As I got older, I started to like

_____

But I still hated

_____

Yum!

Place Photo Here

Yecch!

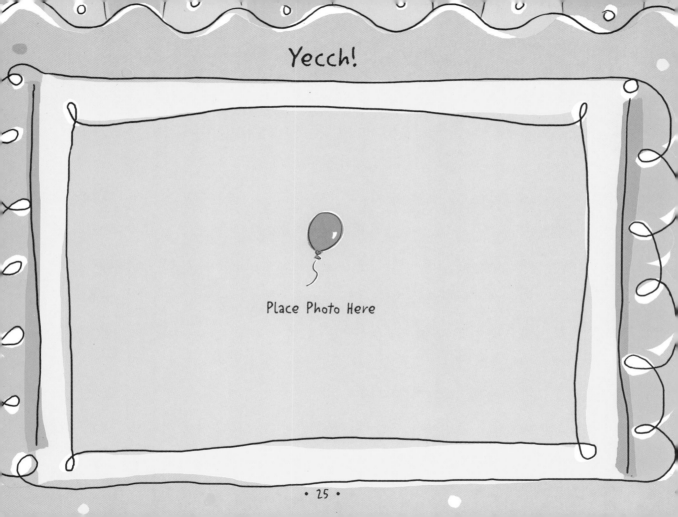

Place Photo Here

How I Grew

First Month _____ Weight _____ Length _____

_____

_____

Second Month _____ Weight _____ Length _____

_____

_____

Third Month _____ Weight _____ Length _____

_____

_____

_____

How I Grew

Fourth Month   Weight   Length

Fifth Month   Weight   Length

Sixth Month   Weight   Length

How I Grew

Seventh Month _____ Weight _____ Length _____

_____

_____

Eighth Month _____ Weight _____ Length _____

_____

_____

Ninth Month _____ Weight _____ Length _____

_____

_____

_____

How I Grew

Tenth Month   Weight   Length
_____

_____

Eleventh Month   Weight   Length
_____

_____

Twelfth Month   Weight   Length
_____

_____

_____

My List of World Records
The first time I...

Smiled
_____

_____

_____

Laughed
_____

_____

_____

Held my head up
_____

_____

_____

Rolled over

_____

_____

_____

Slept through the night (hooray!)

_____

_____

_____

Sat up

_____

_____

_____

Crawled

_____

_____

_____

Smile!

I got my first tooth on _____

_____

☐ It was a breeze   ☐ It was a storm

My other teeth eventually came in on _____
(Dates)

_____

_____

_____

_____

_____

_____

Big Toothy Grin!

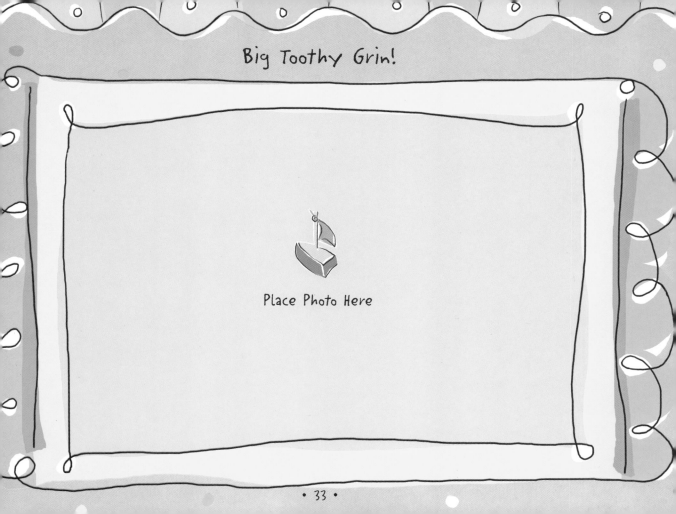

Place Photo Here

My Likes and Dislikes

☐ I was a laid-back baby   ☐ I was a fussbudget

_____

_____

My favorite playtime activity was

_____

_____

My favorite story was

_____

My favorite song was

_____

I'm having some serious fun here!

Place Photo Here

My Likes and Dislikes

In the bath, I liked _____

_____

_____

_____

_____

But I wasn't crazy about _____

_____

_____

_____

_____

Rub a dub, dub . . . Baby in the tub!

Place Photo Here

My Likes and Dislikes

At bedtime, I liked to relax by

_____

_____

_____

But I didn't like to

_____

_____

_____

Place Photo Here

People and Places I Liked to Visit

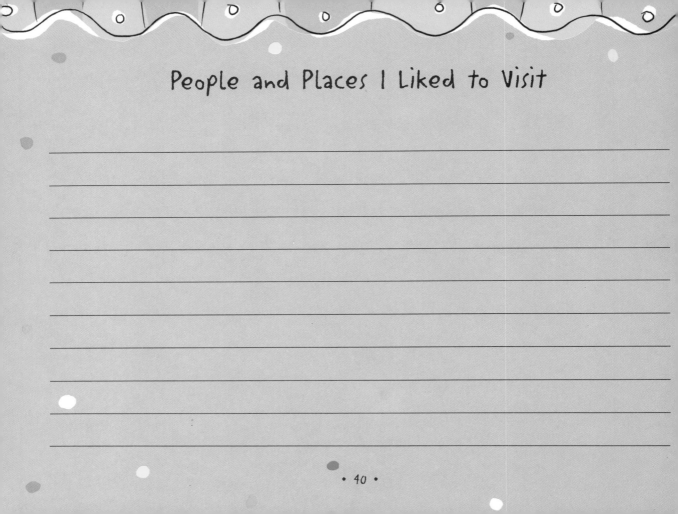

Look at me! I'm the life of the party!

Place Photo Here

My First Holidays

The first holidays I celebrated were

_____

_____

_____

_____

_____

_____

_____

_____

Holiday Baby!

Place Photo Here

One Small Step for Baby . . .

I pulled up to a standing position on

I cruised for the first time on

I took my first steps on

Look what I can do—I'm not a baby any more! I'm a toddler!

Place Photo Here

My First Words of Wisdom

Sounds _____ Date _____

_____

_____

_____

Words _____ Date _____

_____

_____

_____

_____

_____

My First Birthday...I'm a year old!

Photo of First Birthday

My Hand Print

My Foot Print

Date _____

(USE WASHABLE/WATER-BASED PAINT OR INK)